# That Wonderful Redemption

## God's Remedy for Sin

## by Athol Walter

**ISBN: 978-1-78364-239-7**

**www.obt.org.uk**

************

**The Open Bible Trust**

**Fordland Mount, Upper Basildon,**

**Reading, RG8 8LU, UK.**

# That Wonderful Redemption

## Contents

Page

# (1) Introduction

**The question the unbeliever should ask is, "What must I do to be saved?" But ….. the believer should ask, "What did God have to do in order to save me?"**

I was fortunate to be reared in a Christian family, where I not only had Bible stories read to me, but also was given a love and respect for God's Word. Sunday School instruction added to that knowledge. I have since realised, however, that an important part in my instruction had been missed. I cannot remember anyone ever presenting the Bible as a unity, containing coherent and integrated doctrines. It is possible that it was given and I missed it, but I have no recollection of it.

As I've grown older I've started to connect up the Bible stories learned in childhood. It has been a thrilling journey to find that the Bible is not just a collection of bits and pieces, but it has purpose, with themes linked to that purpose, and the more I have come to understand this, the more I understand and value what God has done for me in Christ.

Many people have guided me on my journey. They are far too numerous to mention here, but I must name one because the basic truth this man taught me underlies what I have gained since. Dr. J. Sidlow Baxter, as well as starting me on the dispensational road, taught me that one should synthesize the Scriptures before analyzing them. I had to look up the meaning of synthesize! I had thought that synthetic meant something artificial, or man-made, as opposed to a natural product. I found that to synthesize means to bring a number of things together to make a whole. In other words, Baxter taught me to get the overview first, then look at the details.

As I applied this basic rule, my understanding of God's *Plan of Salvation* grew. I came to see something of the overview and to understand how the parts fitted together. This study is an attempt to put what I learned down on paper, in the hope that it will help others to come to a greater appreciation of what God had to do to bring us salvation. Concentrating on the overview, however, means that some detail will be left out. This booklet is just not big enough. The Open Bible Trust has many publications that enlarge on subjects I have only given little space to, and some are noted on the final pages of this booklet.

I want to emphasise the unity of the Bible. I am struggling for adequate terms to describe what I mean, but God's *Plan of Salvation* is made up of a number of parts, each one being necessary to the success of the whole. Moreover, if any one of the parts is absent or fails, then the whole scheme fails. It is this truth that underlies what I present. Arthur Custance put it very well when he wrote:

> Christian theology is not a system of beliefs loosely thrown together with no essential coherence between the component elements. It is an organic whole, a unified system, a closely connected framework of thought which is logically defensible if preserved in its entirety, but irrational if

merely presented selectively (or piecemeal) as a catalogue of traditional beliefs.

The title for this study comes from a favourite Gospel song of mine, *Tell me the old, old story*, by Katherine Hankey. The second verse says this:

> Tell me the story slowly,
>  that I may take it in,
> That wonderful redemption,
> God's remedy for sin.

We do not need to know and understand all these things in order to be saved. God saves a sinner purely on the basis of faith. But surely understanding should then follow. It must also be said that no matter what we may come to know and understand of God's wonderful redemption, we do not know it all and we cannot answer all the questions. Moreover, there comes a time when all the studying and analyzing must stop, and we simply bow in submission and adoration before our God and Saviour. And perhaps the most appropriate prayer for that moment is found in another much-loved hymn:

Take my life, and let it be consecrated, Lord, to Thee.

# (2)  A prepared body

**"Lo, I come to do thy will, O my God."**

I find myself being drawn to Hebrews 10:5-7 again and again, for the remarkable truth those verses contain. They are a quotation from Psalm 40:6-8. Please compare the two passages.

**Hebrews 10:5-7**
Therefore, when Christ came into the world, he said: "Sacrifice and offering you did not desire, but a body you prepared for me; with burnt offerings and sin offerings you were not pleased. Then I said, 'Here I am – it  is written about me in the scroll – I  have come to do your will, O God.'"

**Psalm 40:6-8**
Sacrifice and offering you did not desire, but my ears you have pierced; burnt offerings and sin offerings you did not require.  Then I said, "Here I am, I have come – it is written about me in the

scroll. I desire to do your will, O my God; your law is within my heart."

In the earlier verses of Hebrews 10, the animal sacrifices of The Law of Moses are contrasted with the Lord Jesus Christ and His once-only sacrifice made in the body prepared for Him. Verse 4 tells us that the animal sacrifices did not wipe out the sins of the people. Rather, they were a continual reminder of sins because they had to be repeated every year. Then come the words that were said when the Word became flesh in order to tabernacle amongst His people:

> "Sacrifice and offering you did not desire, but a body you prepared for me; with burnt offerings and sin offerings you were not pleased. Then I said, "Here I am – it is written about me in the scroll – I have come to do your will, O God."

This is a glimpse of events in Heaven as one of the most important parts of God's *Plan of Salvation* was being put into operation. The long wait of four thousand years was over. The line of Christ's descent had gone from Adam to Abraham and David. Then it divided through two of David's sons and continued on, one line to Joseph, the other to Mary. The two lines then joined in Mary's Boy Child. All was ready and, at the appropriate moment, the Word stooped down from Heaven, inhabited the little body growing in Mary's womb, and was born of the virgin mother in Bethlehem, as the prophets had foretold.

While there was great rejoicing in Heaven, this event went almost unnoticed on earth. But the enemy knew and had his men in place to thwart God's purposes. Nothing, however, can stop God's plans being carried out, and the Gospels record for us the life and teaching of this extraordinary person who is both Son of God and Son of Man.

A striking thing about the Gospels is the number of times that some event or other in the life of Christ is said to fulfil this or that prophecy. I think we can say that His life was scripted for Him, even to His very words. The Lord said a number of times that He spoke not His own words, but only the words that the Father had given Him. Finally, the Father's will brought the Lord to Golgotha.

I had been incorrectly taught about Christ's death as a young Christian. All the emphasis was on the Lord dying 'for me'. Christ died for the sins of the world, I was told, which is certainly true. I was surprised to learn later that He died first of all for the people called the Circumcision; i.e. Israel. Look at Hebrews 2:14-16:

> Since the children have flesh and blood, he too shared in their humanity so that by his death he might destroy him who has the power of death – that is, the devil – and free those who all their lives were held in slavery by their fear of death. For surely it is not angels he helps, but Abraham's descendants.

And consider this verse,

For this reason Christ is the mediator of a new covenant, that those who are called may receive the promised eternal inheritance – now that he has died as a ransom to set them free from the sins committed under the first covenant. (Hebrews 9:15).

And this New Covenant was not made with all mankind, but with the houses of Israel and Judah (Jeremiah 31:31-34).

Don't misunderstand me. I believe without reservation that Christ died for my sins. He took my place, and through His sacrifice I have forgiveness and the promise of eternal life. But I had to learn that the Lord was first of all a minister to the Circumcision (Romans 15:8), and only later did the wider aspects of His sacrificial death become known and available to the rest of the world (1 John 2:22). There is also another reason for Christ's sacrifice that takes precedence even over His death for the people of Israel, but we'll come to that further along.

It is necessary to compare each of the Gospel accounts of the Crucifixion, because they each give emphasis to slightly different aspects of it. An example is the cry the Lord gave just before He died. Matthew, Mark and Luke say that He cried with a loud voice or simply spoke. It is only John who tells us what the Lord cried out (John 19:30). In the Greek text, it is one word, *tetelestai*, which translates into English as "It is finished". We should ask what it was that was finished, because God's whole plan was not complete at that point. It is not till Revelation 21:6 that we find the One seated on the throne saying "It is done." There is also Paul's statement in 1 Corinthians 15:24, which says, "Then the end will come, when (Christ) hands over the Kingdom to God the Father ..." So there was still more to come.

What was finished on the Cross was the Lord's earthly work of becoming the Lamb of God that takes away the sins of the world. But while there was more to come, His death was a goal reached and He could rightly claim to have carried out the will of His Father for which He had come into the world.

While our attention tends to be focused on that riveting sight of the Son of Man on the Cross, we must know that God had traversed a long, hard road to get to that point. So let's turn back now, and try to find out why and where it started.

# (3) Where did sin come from?

### Is it all Adam's fault?

We need to go back before the beginning, as it were. The story does not start with Adam and Eve in Eden. It is true that sin and death came into human experience through Adam's sin, but sin was in the universe before that. The record in the opening chapters of Genesis is rather condensed, to say the least, so we should pay careful attention to what we are told.

At the crucial moment (Genesis 3), a sinister figure in the form of a serpent appears to Eve. We know from what happens later that this figure is Satan, God's enemy and opponent. In Genesis 3, however, no explanation is given as to who this being is, or how he became what he is, or how he came to be in the Garden. His purpose soon becomes clear, for he deceives Eve into doing the one thing that the Lord had said she and Adam were not to do.

Two passages will help us understand Satan better. The first is Ezekiel 28:11-19. The other is Isaiah 14:3-17. In the Ezekiel passage, terms are used that could not be said of any ordinary human being. Consider these:

> You were in Eden, the garden of God; every precious stone adorned you … You were anointed as a guardian cherub, for so I ordained you. You were on the holy mount of God; you walked among the fiery stones. You were blameless in your ways from the day you were created till wickedness was found in you … Your heart became proud on account of your beauty, and you corrupted your wisdom because of your splendour. So I threw you to the earth … By your many sins and dishonest trade you have desecrated your sanctuaries. So I made a fire come out from you, and it consumed you … (Ezekiel 28:11-19)

Not everyone thinks these words refer to Satan, but I do, and through them we are shown how Satan got to the point of wanting for himself the worship that belonged to God alone. This is the origin of sin.

Isaiah 14 gives us more information. Some statements in this passage refer to the King of Babylon, but some, I believe, go beyond him to Satan. Verses 12 to 14 show us just what sin it was that Satan committed. "You said in your heart, 'I will ascend to heaven; I will raise my throne above the stars of God; … I will make myself like the Most High.'" These passages show that Satan was condemned by God and expelled from Heaven for his sin. But some angels sided with Satan. Revelation 12:7 and 9 speak about the dragon and his angels, dragon being another name for Satan.

We must also go to Psalm 8 where David has Adam in mind. He asks in verse 3, "What is man (Adam) that you are mindful of him, the son of man that you care for him? You made him a little lower than the heavenly beings and crowned him with glory and honour." Think about the inference here. Not everyone in Heaven thought Satan was wrong, as we have seen, and it would seem that Satan may have defended himself by saying that anyone in his position would have probably done the same. I can't say that 'rules of conflict' were agreed upon between God and Satan, but from the way the conflict develops, it would seem so. However that may be, the next step in the drama was the creation of Adam, a being lower in status and powers than the angels. I think the inference is that if this lower creature would obey God, then God's action in condemning Satan would be justified.

So let's consider Adam and his place in God's *Plan of Salvation*.

# (4) Who/what was Adam?

**"The first man was of the dust of the earth ..."**

The Bible is silent as to how long the earth was in the shapeless and void state referred to in Genesis 1:2, but when the time was right, God prepared the world for Adam and his descendants.

Genesis informs us that God formed Adam's body out of the dust of the ground, and then breathed into that body the breath or spirit of life. The result was that Adam became a living soul. Please pause here a moment. We are not told that Adam *had* a soul as a result of receiving the breath of life. He *became* a soul. It can be expressed as a simple equation:

**Body + Spirit = Soul**

In other words, the soul is the result of joining body and spirit. Death is just the reverse. When the body and the spirit of life are separated, then the soul dies. I am well aware that the usual belief about this is that humans have an independent soul, a separate part that is everlasting, which goes directly to be with God at the death of a believer. This wrong belief has misled Christendom at large as to what happened in the Garden of Eden, and consequently, as to what happened on Calvary. We'll consider the events of Genesis 3 in the next chapter. For now, we need to see how Adam fits into the scheme.

First of all, Adam was made in the image of God, after His likeness. The Lord Jesus is the Image of God, and Adam was made in the likeness of that Image. Now, if Adam was made in the likeness of the image of God, does that mean that God looks like Adam? No, I don't believe so. What I think it means is that God had already decided what the Man Jesus would look like when He became flesh, and Adam was made in that form.

If you ask me why God did it like this, in the end I would have to say simply, because it pleased Him. But we have already touched on an important clue in Psalm 8:5: "For you made him (that is, Adam) a little lower than the heavenly beings (angels) and you have crowned him with glory and honour." Adam was made a lower being than the angels, because Satan is an angel, and the inference is that if this lower being could withstand temptation and remain obedient to God, then Satan stands condemned.

Genesis has rightly been called the seedbed of the Bible, meaning that the doctrinal truths brought to full flower later grow from seeds germinated in Genesis. So we need to understand that Adam is a picture - the Scriptural word is 'type' – of the Lord Jesus Christ, and indeed, Paul calls the Lord the Last Adam. (1 Corinthians 15:45)

Paul quotes from Psalm 8 in Hebrews 2. In fact, this chapter is almost an exposition of that Psalm. But whereas David had Adam in mind when he penned it, the Holy Spirit has Paul reveal that Psalm 8 really refers to the other

Adam, the Lord Jesus. Notice how the Lord is contrasted with angels in Hebrews 1 and 2. The quote from Psalm 8 starts in verse 6 of Hebrews 2, and in verse 7, we read, "You made him a little lower than the angels; you crowned him with glory and honour and put everything under his feet".

We get the reference to Christ being made lower than the angels again in verse 9, and notice how the glory and honour has been won by Him through His obedience and suffering. What the first Adam lost, the second Adam restored!

Then in Hebrews 2:14 we read that the Lord became human because those He came to help are human. And verse 16 tells us that it was not angels He came to help, but Abraham's descendants. Yes, the Apostle is writing to the Hebrews, so he talks about Abraham and the nation that God built through him, but this does not exclude Gentiles, because Abraham was descended from Noah and ultimately Adam.

The truth we are digging out here is that as the first Adam was made a lower being than an angel, so the last Adam had to be on that same lower plane, to demonstrate that if the lower being could carry out God's Will, then there was no excuse if a higher being did not.

Now, here are some facts about Adam that are essential to God's Plan:

1. Adam was made in the likeness of God's Image; (i.e. in the likeness of Christ).
2. Adam was created sinless, which is not to say that he was righteous for he had not, at that point, been tested. The more accurate word would be innocent.
3. He had the power of choice. He was tested and held accountable for his choice.
4. He was alone.

Each of the above points is significant to the *Plan of Salvation*, but for now, I want to concentrate on the fourth.

When God created humanity on the earth, He started with one man only. While I missed the full significance of this in my early life, Scripture makes a great deal out of it.

In Acts 17:26, when speaking to the Athenians, Paul said, "From one man, He (God) made every nation of men…" The *KJV* translates it as "He hath made of one blood …" Nestlé Greek text just says, "has made of one", there being no noun following. I think that the *NIV* has caught the truth by supplying the word 'man' here, and that one man, of course, is Adam. The Bible also speaks consistently about sin and death coming upon humanity through the sin of that same one man.

It is quite common for us to speak of Adam and Eve as our first parents, which is true. It is important, however, to remember just how God brought Eve into being. She was not created as a separate being, as had been done with Adam. It is a vital part of God's Plan that Eve is out of, or from, Adam.

Let me spell it out. If Eve had been a separate creation from Adam, she would have needed a separate redeemer. The Lord Jesus Christ could not have been her Redeemer, for it is a Scriptural principle that it must be a kinsman who does the redeeming. Eve is "of Adam", in a different way to the rest of us certainly, but nevertheless, because she is of Adam, she is "in Adam" when it comes to God's remedy for sin. There is one other point that needs to be noticed before we move on. This is that Eve did not come under the sentence of death because of Adam's sin. She brought it on herself by her own sin.

When Adam awoke from the sleep into which he had been put, and saw Eve for the first time, he said something very significant. "This is now bone of my bones and flesh of my flesh; she shall be called 'woman' for she was taken out of man." (Genesis 2:23)

So the scene was set. Adam had been created a living soul, a little lower than the angels, and placed in a garden where he had all he needed. He had dominion over all he surveyed, and to cap it all, God provided him with a companion who was bone of his bones and flesh of his flesh. Paradise indeed!

Then came the test!

# (5) What really happened in Genesis 3?

**The events in the Garden of Eden must be viewed as preparatory to Calvary.**

*What did God mean, "You will surely die"?*

The garden into which Adam had been placed had everything that he needed for a fruitful life. There was only one restriction placed on him. The fruit of all the trees in the garden was available except one, for, said God, "You must not eat from the tree of the knowledge of good and evil, for when you eat of it, you will surely die". (Genesis 2:17) Let me say it very clearly. God told Adam – and apparently Adam told Eve – that he could freely eat of everything in the garden except of that one tree, because "if you eat of that tree, Adam, you will die". Then Satan came and said, "You will not die" (Genesis 3:4). Who do you believe?

We can never know for certain what Adam understood God to mean by "die", but why would it mean something different to what we usually think it means? But what I do know is that almost everybody has followed Satan's line, not God's.

We are told by many that this death in Genesis 3 does not mean death as we normally understand it. It is 'spiritual death', or 'separation from God, and don't forget, the soul can't die', they say. It is also said that Adam and Eve started to die that day, which is certainly true.

We hear of deaths from many causes every day and there is not one of us who does not understand that the lives of those involved have been snuffed out. But when it comes to the Bible and spiritual things, we suddenly change and refuse to accept that when God says death, He means death. Whatever you believe on this point, I ask you to keep an open mind while we consider the Scriptures.

Back to Genesis 3. Eve was beguiled by the serpent into tasting the fruit of the forbidden tree. Subsequently, she offered it to Adam, who also ate of it. I don't want to dwell on this, but let's give Adam some credit. A superficial reading might suggest that Adam quite carelessly took and ate of the fruit, but it seems to me that it would have been otherwise. I am not trying to excuse Adam, but I think I can understand to some extent, why he did what he did. When he learned what Eve had done, he knew straight away that he had lost her. What had God said? "The day you eat of the fruit of that tree, you will surely die." This was the woman God had given him, who was part of himself. What would he do if she died and he was left alone? Surely Adam felt as bonded to his mate as we do to ours. Much more so probably, for at this point he was not a fallen being. He loved this woman, and also, I think he knew that God could not give him another Eve.

I suspect that Adam did not lightly choose to eat the fruit, but only did so after agonising over his decision for some time. We don't know how long he took, of course, but one of the reasons why I think Adam had a battle about what he would do, is that the last Adam, also in a garden, had a terrible time agonising over the choice with which He was faced. Whatever the process, we know the choice Adam made. I believe he decided that he could not live without Eve, and if she was to die, he would die with her. In effect, he chose Eve over God.

Then they had to face their Creator and they knew it would not be easy, so they hid themselves. They also had become conscious of their nakedness and made skirts out of leaves to cover themselves. More on this shortly.

Before we go on, let me ask you a question. God had said that if they ate of the forbidden fruit, they would die that day. Did Adam and Eve die that day? What do you think?

The Lord came into the garden late in the day, as was His habit, and called the pair to Him. The sorry tale came out bit by bit, and in verse 14 and 15, we have the Lord's words to the serpent. Verse 15 is the important part for us. "And I will put enmity between you and the woman, and between your offspring and hers; he will crush your head, and you will strike his heel."

## *Punishment or consequence?*

Before considering whether Adam and Eve died that day, I want to discuss the subject of death a little more.

I think that many of God's directions to us about how to live are given because of the inevitable consequences of certain actions. When He warns us against certain behaviour, He is not trying to stop us enjoying ourselves. Rather, He knows that bad consequences come from such things, so tells us not to live that way.

We parents do exactly the same with our children. We know what they don't understand at a young age. There is danger on the street, so we tell them not to run out on the street. They fret about it, because they think we are just being mean, and we all know of children who have ignored or forgotten their parents' instructions, run out onto the street and suffered as a consequence.

Then there is another aspect to it. As well as warning our children that if they go on the street they might get hurt, we might also tell them that if they disobey, we will punish them in some way. My point is that the punishment, whatever it might be, is different from any consequences that might follow the child's disobedience. We need to realise that there was a punishment component, as well as consequences, when God said, "In the day you eat of the fruit of that tree, you will die."

It seems to me that Christian expositors have taken God's words here to be all about consequences, without any thought of punishment in them at all, so the emphasis is on the idea of Adam and Eve starting to die that day, the process continuing for hundreds of years in their cases, until finally their bodies surrendered and gave up their spirits.

I want to put it to you as strongly as I can, however, that the process of death, which did indeed start in them on that day, was a *consequence*, but that God had also meant that they would die that very day, as punishment for their disobedience.

### *Did Adam and Eve die that day?*

What was your answer? Here is mine. I believe the answer is "Yes and no!" It looks like I want to have it both ways, doesn't it? Let's think about it.

As we saw earlier, the Lord told the serpent that the woman's offspring would destroy him. We are not told what Adam and Eve thought when they heard these words, but they must have been a bit confused, to say the least. It sounded as if there might be some hope. Maybe they were not going to die after all.

After speaking to the serpent and also Adam and Eve, the Lord then did something which I think is at the heart of the whole drama. It's in Genesis 3:21. "The Lord God made garments of skin for Adam and his wife and clothed them".

If I changed my question slightly, maybe you would have given a different answer, so let me rephrase it. Were there any deaths in the Garden that day? I hope you answer yes to that. The Lord made garments out of skins, and for years, it never occurred to me to ask where He got the skins from. It's obvious once the right question is asked. Two animals died that day as substitutes for Adam and Eve, which is why I say that yes, they did die, and yet on the other hand, they did not die that day, because they lived on for hundreds of years.

I find it exciting that here, at the dawn of human history, the Gospel is clearly presented, if we but have the eyes to see it. The doctrine of substitutionary sacrifice is proclaimed hard on the heels of Adam's disobedience. The aprons of leaves that these two made for themselves were not sufficient, for "without the shedding of blood there is no remission". The blood of the animals slain to provide the 'coverings' for the guilty pair points forward to the blood of the true Lamb of God that takes away the sins of the world. I believe that the reference to Christ as "The Lamb that was slain from the foundation of the world" (Revelation 13:8) reaches right back to that very moment in the Garden of Eden.

To summarise then, so no one will be in any doubt as to what I am suggesting: God created Adam as a lower being to angels and placed him in a garden where he had everything he needed. His mate, Eve, was made in such a way that, although she was different - female to his male - she was, nevertheless, of or from Adam. They were both innocent and without sinful natures. God placed one restriction upon them as a test. Satan, God's adversary, tempted Eve and deceived her into eating the forbidden fruit. This was how he got to Adam. When Adam saw what his wife had done, he chose to eat the fruit and die with her, rather than live alone without 'the woman whom God had given Him'.

They expected to die that same day as a punishment for their disobedience, but instead they heard the Lord pronounce words of hope, promising a Redeemer who would destroy Satan. Other punishments and consequences were also pronounced on them and on the serpent. Then the

Lord killed two animals and provided Adam and Eve with garments of skins to cover them. So while they did not physically die that day, they died typically in the deaths of their substitutes, all of which parallels the deaths of believers in Christ when faith is exercised in the true, as opposed to the typical, Lamb of God. While they were not executed that day, sin and death had started to operate in their bodies, and eventually they did die.

So Adam and Eve were saved from immediate punishment, but were they 'really saved'?

# (6) Is Christ the Saviour of all men?

**"… we have put our hope in the living God, who is the Saviour of all men, and especially of those who believe".  (1 Timothy 4:10)**

The verse above is one of a number of Scripture passages that have caused me problems over the years. When I first actually noticed what it said, I was rather taken aback. I had thought that the Lord was the Saviour of *only* those who believed, but suddenly, here was a verse telling me that God was the Saviour of all men, and especially of those who believed. The answer came with a correct understanding of Genesis 3.

We have seen that the Lord provided a way out for Adam and Eve. They had not known about it, and the Lord could not have told them about it beforehand. It was only after they disobeyed God that they learned that the animal sacrifices protected them from their immediate punishment. But were they saved in the same

*That Wonderful Redemption*                                    38

way that a believer in Christ is saved now? I don't believe so, yet it is still correct to say they were saved.

Have you ever wondered how the Lord could continue relating to Adam and Eve after they sinned? Certainly He said very different things to them after their sin than before, but how could God, whose Holiness cannot tolerate sin at all, continue to have dealings with them when they became sinners? We could also profitably ask how God can relate to us, even though we know that we are still sinners. The answer lies 'in the Blood', to use an evangelical phrase. Not only is the Lord Jesus called the Lamb slain *from* the foundation of the world, but He is also called the Lamb fore-ordained *before* the foundation of the world (Revelation 13:8; 1 Peter 1:19,20). It is the consistent testimony of Scripture that it is only on the basis of the shed blood of that fore-ordained Lamb that God can have dealings with sinful humanity.

What the 'shed blood' did for Adam and Eve in the Garden, was to suspend the sentence. What was the benefit in that? Apart from averting their executions, which I'm sure they thought was beneficial, it gave them time to repent and accept the life that was being offered to them. Consider this verse from Genesis 6:3.

> Then the Lord said, "My Spirit will not contend with man forever, for he is mortal; his days will be a hundred and twenty years."

I am aware of various interpretations of this verse but one seems to have been overlooked. Notice that the word 'man' in the verse is 'Adam' in the Hebrew. I know that 'Adam' is often used for humanity in general, as well as referring to the first man. The time span of 120 years may refer to the number of years from that point to the flood, but it cannot mean the lifespan of humanity in general, as is sometimes suggested, for we read of many who lived for much longer than that in succeeding chapters. If, however, the verse does refer to the man Adam, then it is saying that God's Spirit is not going to contend with Adam forever, and that he has only another 120 years to go before his death.

Did Adam ever repent and place his life in the hands of a loving God? I don't know, but if the Spirit was contending with Adam for all those years, it makes me wonder. The immediate sentence of death had been suspended because of the typical sacrifice. This gave him time - a long time in his case - to consider his position, but we do not know whether he ever took the next step of faith.

This, then, is how God is the Saviour of all men without reference to whether they have believed the Gospel or not. The blood of the Lamb of God, who died for the sins of the world, holds up the sentence of death on all humanity, to give all the chance to repent and believe the Gospel. Those who do so receive the promise of eternal life through Christ, and are no longer under the death sentence. Those who do not, are saved in the meantime from the sentence of immediate death, but when the time comes for them to stand before their Judge, the sentence will be carried out.

Romans 5:18 is similar to 1 Timothy 4.10. It reads: "Consequently, just as the result of one trespass was condemnation for all men, so also the result of one act of righteousness was justification that brings life for all men." We well know that all people do not have life in Christ, for many refuse to believe the Gospel, but the one act of righteousness, i.e. the sinless One becoming sin for the rest of us, gains for the all who are in the first Adam, the opportunity of entering life purchased by the last Adam.

To make the story complete, we should also note that it is the teaching of Scripture that the fallen nature, which started to operate in Adam and Eve the day they sinned, has been passed down to all of Adam's descendants (Romans 5:13-18).

Except One!

# (7) God's problem.

**"Who can bring a clean thing out of an unclean?" (Job 14:4, KJV)
You cannot make something clean without making something else dirty.**

I came across the above quote recently in a magazine, which had nothing to do with the Bible, yet it is a profound theological truth. Then I realised that the converse is also true, viz.:-

**You cannot use something that is dirty
to make something else clean.**

These quotes are so simple, yet so profound, and they bring us the problem God had in dealing with sin. In one sense, it sounds a little silly to say that God has a problem with anything. He is, after all, the Almighty, the Creator of heaven and earth, and within the confines of His character, can do anything. So what's the problem? Just this.

God had to provide a solution to sin that first of all met every demand of His Holiness without compromising Himself. Secondly, it had to wipe the slate clean for every offender and allow each one to be dealt with simply on the basis of their acceptance or refusal of His offered forgiveness. Thirdly, the solution must make it transparently obvious to all, particularly the angelic host in Heaven, that justice had been done. As Paul says in Romans 3:26, "He did it to demonstrate his justice at the present time, so as to be just ..."

God's *Plan of Salvation* involved God Himself coming into the world in a form in which the punishment for sin could be paid. The One who would pay the price had to be a kinsman-redeemer. In other words, the redeemer had to be one of the family. We will discuss that in the next chapter.

It was not enough for God simply to appear in a human form. There could be no make-believe, as it were. The Redeemer had to be truly human. And this is where God's problem lies.

The quote from Job at the beginning of the chapter sums it up very well. "How can a clean thing come from an unclean?" There is another verse, Job 25:4, which needs to be noted. "How then can a man be righteous before God? *How can one born of woman be pure*?" The questions are rhetorical. We all know immediately that the answer is that no one born of woman in the normal way can be pure or clean.

But God had a solution to the problem that would not compromise Him in any way. We get the first hint about it in Genesis 3:15. Let me quote just the relevant parts. "I will put enmity between ... your offspring and her (offspring); he (i. e. the woman's offspring) will crush your (i.e. Satan's) head, and you (Satan) will strike his heel." As you will know, the *KJV* renders 'the offspring of the woman' as 'the seed of the woman', which I think is more accurate, so I will use that phrase.

Visualise the scene. There is the background of the garden. There are four characters, viz. the Lord, the serpent, Adam and Eve. Did the Lord push Adam into the background as He spoke of the seed of the woman? Maybe He just gestured towards Eve as He spoke. However it happened, the words are very specific. It is the seed of the woman, the woman's descendant, not the seed of the man, who will destroy the serpent.

The next hint that God gives of His way of overcoming the problem is found in Isaiah 7:14. "Therefore the Lord himself will give you a sign: The virgin will be with child and will give birth to a son and will call him Immanuel." These are words of the Lord, through Isaiah, to King Ahaz. I think that this sign had an initial fulfilment then and meant something to Ahaz, but neither he nor Isaiah knew the deeper meaning behind the prophecy. But we know, for Matthew 1:22,23 tells us, "All this took place to fulfil what the Lord had said through the prophet: The virgin will be with child and will give birth to a son, and they will call him Immanuel". *Immanuel* is a Hebrew word that means "God with us."

The Scriptures are clear that Mary's baby was indeed without the stain of Adam's sin. In Luke 1:35, we read of the angel's visit to Mary.

Notice that in the preceding couple of verses, after the angel tells Mary she will become pregnant and give birth to a son, she asks the very relevant question, "How will this be since I am a virgin?" The angel answers, "The Holy Spirit will come upon you, and the power of the most high will overshadow you. So the *Holy One* to be born will be called the son of God." Don't miss the significance of the 'so'. It means, 'therefore' or 'because of this'.

God's solution, then, is the "virgin birth". To be accurate, we should speak of the virgin *conception*, for the birth was perfectly natural. It was *the conception that was unique* and which provided the means by which this baby alone, of all babies ever born, could be called the 'Holy One'. As we have seen earlier, it is the man who started the process of passing on the sinful nature to the next generation, and it is the father, in each case, who passes it on, *not the mother*.

If you react negatively to that, let me point out that God was able to use one of Mary's natural ova to be the source for the body prepared for the Lord of Glory. If the ova of the woman carried the sinful nature, then God could not have used a woman at all. I have seen the objection raised that the ova of women must be tainted by sin as well as everything else in their bodies, and therefore God planted a special egg in Mary's womb. It sounds a good idea until it is examined. If the egg from which the baby Jesus grew was not Mary's natural egg, and Mary was used as a human incubator, then the Lord was not Mary's son, and therefore He was not descended from David or Abraham, and most importantly of all, He was not descended from Adam. If that is true, it means that He would be neither Adam's kinsman-redeemer, nor ours.

So, to repeat the point because it is so important: the Lord used Mary's natural egg, but He would not let Joseph have any part in this conception at all. The Holy Spirit miraculously fertilised Mary's egg, so that on the one hand, this Baby was rightfully, but in a special way, the Son of Man, and on the other hand, He was also truly the Son of God. Also, this was the way in which He was the Seed of the Woman.

I want to mention one other point here. Hebrews 10:5 says: "Therefore, when Christ came into the world, he said, 'Sacrifice and offering you did not desire, but a body you prepared for me.'" In our discussion so far, we have seen how God overcame the problem of bringing the Redeemer into the world as a real human being, and yet not having the fallen nature that the rest of us are blighted with. The word 'prepared' in the verse just quoted means more than just getting something ready. It means to be prepared especially so as to be entirely suitable for its purpose. I hope you can now see something of the way in which this particular body was so thoroughly suitable for the Word (Christ) to inhabit. Remember, we are speaking of the Word who created everything. And yet this same Creator humbled Himself, entered into Mary's womb and was born of a woman.

# (8) The Kinsman-Redeemer.

## One of the family.

There are two questions that should be answered by anyone considering God's wonderful Redemption.

(1)   Why did Christ have to be born?

And

(2)   Why did Christ have to die?

The second question partly answers the first. The Word had to become flesh in order die, because God cannot die. It was also necessary for the One who would be the Redeemer of lost humanity to be a member of that humanity Himself. We do not have to go far to find the reason for this. Hebrews 10, which we have already looked at, makes it quite clear that it is impossible for the blood of bulls and goats to take away sins. Why? Because a man's sins must be paid for with the man's life. A bull, no matter how magnificent an animal it might be, is not a human, so cannot stand in a human's place. But another human can - with one proviso: the substitute must have no sins of his own to pay for!

While it is not entirely foreign to western culture, in eastern cultures it has been the rule that if someone is to be rescued from debt, prison or slavery, or if a death or some other wrong is to be avenged, then the one who does the redeeming/avenging must be as close a relative as possible. This is also the Scriptural principle.

We find it illustrated in Genesis 14. Abraham's nephew, Lot, was carried off by a band of marauders. When Uncle Abraham heard of it, he rounded up as many men as he could and set off in pursuit. He rescued Lot and the other captives, returning with a large amount of booty. Read the chapter for the details. The important point for us is that Abraham did not hesitate to fulfil his obligation as Lot's kinsman, regardless of the danger to himself.

The principle is set out more fully in the Book of Ruth. Please read it right through, because we can only look at the relevant parts for this study.

The record opens in Bethlehem, which means 'house of bread'. The meanings of the names throughout are significant, but I will leave you to look them up for yourself. But despite the meaning of the name, there is a severe famine in the land, and Elimelech, Naomi's husband, takes his family to Moab, because he has heard that there is food there. Although things seem to go well at first, and the two sons marry Moabite girls, disaster strikes.

Elimelech and his two sons die and Naomi is left with her two daughters-in-law. She decides to go back to her own country. She tells the two younger women to return to the homes of their fathers as she has no more sons to marry them. One girl does go back, but the other, Ruth, will not leave her mother-in-law, and makes one of the most moving speeches in Scripture as she declares her commitment (Ruth 1:16,17).

The two women return to Bethlehem where things aren't much better, for they have to rely on begging for sustenance. There is also the matter of no sons in the family to preserve the family's land. It is the time of harvest, and Naomi sends Ruth out to glean in the fields. This means that she, with other poor women, would follow the reapers in a field and pick up any stalks of the crop that the reapers left behind. Ruth happened to go into the field of a man called Boaz, who took a liking to her. He told his reapers to leave extra pickings for her, and not to harass her. Naomi was surprised when Ruth returned with more grain than might be expected, but she was delighted when Ruth told her where she had been gleaning. She said, "That man is our close relative; he is one of our kinsman-redeemers" (2:20).

Naomi later instructs Ruth to act in a way that sounds strange to us (Ruth 3), but it was in accordance with their customs, and did not involve any improper conduct. Ruth was to go to the threshing floor at night where Boaz was sleeping. She then was to lie at his feet and get under the corner of the blanket. When Boaz awoke and asked who was there, she told him, and then said, "Spread the corner of your garment over me, since you are a kinsman-redeemer." This was a request for Boaz to marry her, in order to raise up a son for her dead husband, so their inheritance could be preserved and their place in Israel assured.

Boaz knew exactly what Ruth was asking. But there is a stumbling block. See Boaz' words in 3:12, "Although it is true that I am near of kin, there is a kinsman-redeemer nearer than I." This was a problem, for the nearer kinsman had the prior claim. But Boaz continued, "Stay here for the night, and in the morning if he wants to redeem, good; let him redeem. But if he is not willing, as surely as the Lord lives, I will do it. Lie here until morning."

Ruth chapter 4 tells how Boaz approached his relative, who said he would redeem Elimelech's property. Then Boaz told his relative that when he bought the property, he would also get Ruth the Moabitess, who came with it. At this, the relative backed out, leaving the field to Boaz. So Boaz redeemed the property and married Ruth. The book closes with a wonderful little family tree. Ruth's son was Obed; Obed's son was Jesse and, of course, Jesse's youngest son was David, who became the King of Israel. Turn to the Gospels of Matthew and Luke and you can follow the line right down to Mary's son, born in Bethlehem, of the line of David, and Abraham … and Adam.

Boaz is a type of Christ as the Kinsman-redeemer, and the Redeemer had to be the nearest kinsman possible.

The different threads of our overall study are now starting to come together. The Lord told Satan in Eden, that it would be the Seed of the woman, the woman's offspring, who would destroy him. This was said before there was ever any tradition about kinsman-redeemers, but the custom was later developed and was well understood.

Our Kinsman-Redeemer had to be born without the sinful nature if He was to stand in our place. God had circumvented this problem by the conception of Jesus being brought about by the power of God, without the participation of a human father.

Let's pause for a moment. I have emphasised the unity of Christian doctrine and the necessity for all the foundational truths to be present and correct. As Custance again says so eloquently, "if we abandon any single part of the revelation of Scripture, we make shipwreck of the whole plan of redemption". It is not uncommon to hear not only rank and file Christians, but also Christian leaders, say that they do not believe the doctrine of the 'virgin birth'. They don't seem to realise that by throwing this truth out, the whole fabric of Gospel truth goes with it.

The Bible is adamant that the Lord Jesus Christ was like Adam in every respect except one. The Lord was *without sin* and the language of Scripture carefully safeguards this truth. Unfortunately, the exactness does not always carry over into English translations. I can't do better than quote several texts, but first, let me remind you again that it was to be the seed of the woman, not the seed of the man, who would bring about Satan's downfall.

> ... and Jacob the father of Joseph, the husband of Mary, of whom was born Jesus, who is called Christ. (Matthew 1:16)

> "... Joseph, son of David, do not be afraid to take Mary home as your wife, because what is conceived in her is from the Holy Spirit." (Matthew 1:20. Read the context. Joseph knew full well that he was not the father of Mary's expected child!)

> "How will this be", Mary asked the angel, "since I am a virgin?" The angel answered, "The Holy Spirit will come upon you, and the power of the Most High will overshadow you. So the holy one to be born will be called the Son of God. ... For nothing is impossible with God." (Luke 1:34,35,37)

*That Wonderful Redemption*

Now Jesus himself was about thirty years old when he began his ministry. He was the son, so it was thought, of Joseph. (Luke 3:23)

For what the law was powerless to do in that it was weakened by the sinful nature, God did by sending his own Son in the likeness of sinful man to be a sin offering. (Romans 8:3)
God made him who had no sin to be sin for us, so that in him we might become the righteousness of God. (2 Corinthians 5:21)

I would like to paraphrase that last verse in the words of the quote I used in the previous chapter.

God made Him who was clean to be dirty for us, so that we (who were dirty) might have God's cleanliness in Him.

Are they not sweet words?

# (9) What really happened in the other garden?

**Was it only the first Adam who had the power of choice?**

I have emphasised the parallels between the two men Scripture calls Adam, in other words, between Adam and the Lord Jesus, the last Adam. Therefore, I think it is no accident that as the Lord's hour approaches, we find Him in a garden where events occur that are as consequential for humanity as those that took place in the garden of Eden, if not more so.

The Lord had been tested early in His earthly ministry, but on the eve of His crucifixion, He is to be tested to the limit. The question He must answer is the same one that both Satan and Adam answered wrongly. That question is, "Will You obey the Father's wil completely, or choose Your own will against the Father's?"

Several things must be borne in mind as we consider Gethsemane. I know I am repeating myself, but firstly, the Lord went through this test as a real man. If He was God just pretending to be a man, then Adam does not have a case to answer. Secondly, He was sinless. He was not only born without the fallen nature, but had not sinned during His life. He challenged His opponents to find any sin in Him. Thirdly, He also knew that He was not only to be the sacrificial Lamb, typically carrying the sins of the world, but that He would *actually become sin*. This can only mean that the Lord took on Himself every sin of Adam and his descendants, as if He had done them all. And herein, I believe, lies the greatest horror that the Lord was called upon to face. The awfulness of it really is beyond our comprehension, but this is what caused His agony as He prayed in Gethsemane, more so than the contemplation of the coming physical suffering.

I know that many will disagree with my interpretation of Gethsemane, but I can only tell it as I see it. The question is whether the Lord could have refused to carry out the Father's will. Some say that He could not have refused, that it is unthinkable that He even had the thought, and the test was only to show His true character. This seems to me to ignore a number of passages, which we will come to shortly.

Notice what the Lord prayed in the Garden. "Father, if you are willing, take this cup from me; yet not my will, but yours be done" (Luke 22:42). Matthew and Mark vary slightly, but are essentially the same. It seems to me that the Lord was saying very strongly that He did not want to walk the path laid out for Him, but if there could be no other way, then He would drink the cup. And drink it He did.

Now what are the Scriptures that bear on whether the Lord had any choice or not?

Hebrews 5:8: "Although he was a son, he learned obedience from what he suffered."

Philippians 2:8: "And being found in appearance as a man, he humbled himself and became obedient to death – even death on a cross!"

If Christ had no choice in whether He went to the Cross, then it is pointless to say that He was obedient. Obedience only has meaning in contrast to disobedience. To my mind, to say that the Lord had a choice, and could have refused to obey His Father, does not detract either from Himself, His character, or what He did. On the contrary, I think it makes His actions more wonderful.

I believe that much revolves around the contrast between the man Adam and the man Jesus. The Plan of Redemption necessitated that the Lord be on exactly the same footing as Adam when Adam was tested in Eden. Do you remember the various points I made about Adam back in chapter 3? See how each one is true of Christ also.

1. He is the Image of God. (Adam was the likeness of the Image.)
2. He was sinless.
3. He had the power of choice, and was tested as to His obedience. Just as great and terrible things flowed from Adam's choice, so great and wonderful things flowed from the Lord's choice.
4. He was alone. As it was Adam alone – not Eve – who carried the burden of responsibility, so the Lord Jesus was the only one who could pay the price for Adam's sin and all that flowed from it, and bring God's wonderful Plan to its full fruition. I should also remind you that as the first Adam was said to be made lower than the angels, so is the last Adam. So Satan is condemned.

Back in Gethsemane, no sooner was the battle won, than the Temple police arrived to arrest Him. He submitted, as the prophets foretold, and was led away to humiliation, abuse and death.

# (10) Paid in full.

**In the Old Testament we do not get reasoned theology, but illuminated experience.**

Rather than concentrate on the details of the Crucifixion now, I want to touch on some things which illuminate those events for us, and take us behind them to the deeper significance.

The Old Testament teaches God's Truth through people and events – illuminated experience. We find one of the 'illuminating experiences' about Calvary in Genesis 22 where we read of Abraham offering Isaac to God.

This is a wonderful picture of the love of the Father in providing His Son as the Lamb that takes away the sins of the world. It also shows the willingness of the Son to submit to the Father's will. As I think about Abraham's feelings as he journeys with Isaac to the place which God would show him, it helps me to understand a little of what God the Father went through as He went with His Son to the place of sacrifice on one of the same hills of Moriah, if not the very same.

Notice verses 6 and 8: "And the two of them went on together." This is what happened at the Crucifixion – the Father and the Son, leaving everyone behind, and going on together to the place of darkness and death. But the point came with Abraham and Isaac, when the father, who loved his son, had to become the executioner. At that point Isaac was alone. In the same way, the moment came on that Hill called Calvary, when the Father laid on His blameless Son the iniquity of us all and had to turn away from His beloved Son. No wonder darkness came over the scene.

We will never know this side of resurrection exactly what took place during those three hours of darkness, but it was something that no one was allowed to witness. Can you imagine the intensity of suffering behind the cry that was torn from our Saviour as He suffered there, "My God, my God, why have you forsaken Me?" Was there some similar cry, or at least similar thought, in Isaac's mind, as he saw his father lift the knife above him? While Isaac may not have understood what was happening, the Lord knew exactly what was to come, but in spite of that, what He suffered there brought from Him that heart-wrenching cry of despair.

But there was another cry to follow. No longer despair and a feeling of abandonment, now it's the triumphant "It is finished." As I mentioned before the Greek word is *tetelestai*, and archaeological discoveries about the end of the 19<sup>th</sup> century have given added significance to the word. It certainly means "It is finished", but amongst the documents found, most of them written in the very style of Greek used in the New Testament, were many statements of account, showing what various people owed to different traders etc. And across these accounts was written the word *tetelestai*. It obviously had the meaning of "Paid in Full", and every believer should be grateful that God has stamped across the statement of our sins, "Paid in Full".

Many benefits flow from the Lord's death on the Cross, not the least of which is the forgiveness of sins and life in Christ which we enjoy every day of our lives. However, unless something more important had been accomplished by the Lord's death first, all the blessings which are ours in Christ would not have come about.

So let's find out what that more important thing is.

# (11) The Atonement.

## What is it and who gets it?

I said in an earlier chapter that there was another reason for the death of Christ other than our redemption, and we come to it now. A number of terms are used both in Scripture and in evangelical circles, to describe the various results of the Lord's death, and we are often rather careless in our understanding and use of these terms. I refer to such words as:

- redemption,
- forgiveness,
- reconciliation,
- salvation,
- sanctification and
- atonement (the one I want to focus on now).

It is important to understand right away that we, the believers, do not receive the Atonement. I know that Romans 5:11 in the *KJV* says that we have received the atonement. Later translations change the word to 'reconciliation'. When the *KJV* was translated, the word atonement was used in two ways, firstly, to make amends for some wrong done, and secondly, to make at one two people who had become alienated. So, to at-one meant to reconcile. This secondary meaning has dropped out of modern English usage.

To be clear, Paul was not saying in Romans 5:11 that we receive the atonement, meaning that the Lord's death somehow made amends to us for some wrong done to us. What he meant was that, as a result of the Lord's sacrifice, we do receive the reconciliation. In other words, we who were once alienated from God because of sin, have been made 'at-one' with Him.

So who gets the atonement? In the matter of sin, who is the offended party? Not us. We are the offending party! Whose law has been broken by sin? Again, not ours. There is only one answer. It is God whose Law has been broken and who is offended by sin. And before any blessing or benefit can flow to any other party, full and sufficient atonement must be made to God for that offence.

The Lord's cry on the Cross, *tetelestai,* or "Paid in Full", should conjure up in our minds the thought of a debt owed. What debt? A life. Think of Adam again back in Eden. "Don't eat that fruit, Adam, or you will die." He ate the fruit, but the sentence of death was suspended because of the substitute that died in his place, even though it was an animal. But a debt had been incurred, and Adam's natural death some 900 years later did not pay it off. It had to be death as a punishment. It was not until the last Adam voluntarily gave His life that the debt was paid in full. When that happened, the wrong was amended and the offence caused by the breaking of God's Law was removed. In other words, atonement was made to God. Then, all the blessings which are so important to us, can flow freely out from the heart of God who is not only love, but holiness as well.

2 Corinthians 5 has some pertinent verses on this subject. From verse 18, Paul speaks of the ministry of reconciliation given to him by God.

"All this is from God, who reconciled us to himself through Christ and gave us the ministry of reconciliation: that God was reconciling the world to himself in Christ, not counting men's sins against them. ...We implore you on Christ's behalf: Be reconciled to God."

Notice the order in which God's Plan progressed. As the *KJV* puts it, God was in Christ, reconciling the world to Himself. That had to be first. The demands of God's holy Law had to be met and satisfied, otherwise any move on His part to forgive sin would compromise Him. So the first result of the Lord's death was to pay the price and remove the sin's offence. In other words, Christ made atonement to God. This reconciled God to the world, and allowed the wonderful message to go out to those who would hear it, "God is now reconciled to you. Come you, and be reconciled to God."

The truth is that there is no limitation whatsoever to the Atonement that the death of the Lord Jesus Christ provided, as some teach. It lays down the unquestionable and unshakeable foundation for that wonderful redemption which

God has offered to all humanity. God, of course, knows those who are His from the beginning, but the offer of salvation is to all. Not everyone responds to the Gospel and believes, and for that they will answer to the One whom God has appointed as Judge. And who is that Judge? Not the Father, who was not born of the virgin, but the Son, the One who was born and became part of the human family, who learned the cost of obedience through the things that He suffered, and so earned the right to be our Judge.

For those of us who have held out our hand in faith and taken hold of God's lifeline, we can rest assured that when the Lord judges our walk, it will be done with an understanding sympathy, for He walked the human road. For those, however, who reject the ministry of reconciliation, resurrection will bring them to the judgement where the price of that rejection will be demanded. The Bible calls that price the second death from which there is no resurrection (Revelation 20:12-15).

# (12) Untouched by death.

**When death confronts us, death wins.**
**When Christ confronted death, death lost.**

It came as quite a shock to me, when, as a teenager, I first read Psalm 22. I don't know how I had missed it before, but when I read the opening words, "My God, my God, why have you forsaken me?" I at least knew to which event those words applied. It is amazing that Psalm 22 quite graphically describes crucifixion, yet that particular form of death was still to be invented centuries later. Verses 16 and 17 are especially accurate of the Lord's Crucifixion.

> Dogs have surrounded me; a band of evil men has encircled me, they have pierced my hands and my feet. I can count all my bones; people stare and gloat over me. They divide my garments among them and cast lots for my clothing.

But let's settle first, that the guilt of that contemporary generation of Israel is established beyond doubt by the New Testament record.

> When Pilate saw that he was getting nowhere, but that instead an uproar was starting, he took water and washed his hands in front of the crowd, "I am innocent of this man's blood," he said. "It is your responsibility!" All the people answered, "Let his blood be on us and on our children!" (Matthew 27: 24, 25)

> But they shouted, "Take him away! Take him away! Crucify him!" "Shall I crucify your king?" Pilate asked. "We have no king but Caesar,' the chief priests answered." (John 19: 15)

> "Therefore let all Israel be assured of this: God has made this Jesus, whom you crucified, both Lord and Christ." (Acts 2:36)

"You killed the author of life, but God raised him from the dead. We are witnesses of this." (Acts 3:15)

"… then know this, you and all the people of Israel: It is by the name of Jesus Christ of Nazareth, whom you crucified but whom God raised from the dead, that this man stands before you healed." (Acts 4:10)

So, on the one hand, that favoured generation of Israel put their Messiah to death. But, on the other hand, the Lord had said very clearly that no man would take His life from Him. He would lay it down Himself. "The reason my Father loves me is that I lay down my life – only to take it up again. No one takes it from me, but I lay it down of my own accord. I have authority to lay it down and authority to take it up again. This command I received from my Father" (John 10:17, 18).

These two facts are the reason why crucifixion was chosen for the Lord's death. It is crucifixion alone, of the various forms of execution available, that allows for these two different aspects. The Jews crucified Him, without doubt intending to kill Him, and therefore could be rightfully charged with His murder. But they did not take His life from Him, for He chose the moment when He died.

Again we must take care, for our English translations don't bring out the point. Matthew says that the Lord gave up His spirit. We find the same in Mark and Luke, who say that Jesus breathed His last. As far as these three writers were concerned, it was a passive thing. Death happened to the Lord. But John is different. He uses a different word, a word which means that the Lord commanded His spirit to leave, which is something none of us can ever do. He commanded Himself to die, and die He did. In truth, He laid down His life, no one taking it from Him. But please notice, that because crucifixion did not bring about the immediate death of the victim, the Lord had time to undergo all that was necessary during the three hours of darkness, to satisfy every demand of od's Holiness in dealing with sin.

So the work was done. The debt was cleared in full. God's Holiness and Justice were fully satisfied. The Veil of the Temple was split from top to bottom and henceforth, those in Christ have unhindered access into the presence of God.

When death confronts us, we lose. Death wins. When death confronted Christ, He won. Death lost.

Now, to the next step. Look at these verses:

Therefore my heart is glad and my tongue rejoices; my body also will rest secure, because you will not abandon me to the grave, nor will you let your Holy One see decay. (Psalm 16:9, 10)

Peter uses these verses, and more, in his address in Acts 2, but I want to go to Acts 13. In verse 35, Paul also quotes the statement that the Lord would not see decay, and then in verse 37, he says this,

"But the one whom God raised from the dead did not see decay. Therefore, my brothers, I want you to know that through Jesus the forgiveness of sins is proclaimed to you."

Note the 'therefore'. He says that the forgiveness of sins is a 'therefore' coming out of the fact that the Lord's body did not see corruption or decay in the grave. It is an important point. We well know how quickly the body of a dead animal starts to smell. But it was different with the Lord. There was no sin in His body for death to work on. Our bodies are in a state of decay even while we live, and when we die, the body's breakdown is very rapid. But not with the Holy One of God.

The death of Lazarus in John 11 shows the contrast. When the Lord heard that Lazarus was sick, He deliberately waited another two days before He told His disciples they were going to Bethany. We'll come to the reason for that in a moment.

When He arrived at Bethany and was taken to where Lazarus had been interred, the Lord commanded that the tomb be opened. Martha was horrified. "But, Lord, by this time there is a bad odour, for he has been there four days." I rather like the directness of the *KJV* translation which has Martha saying that by this time he stinks. The Greek text says simply, "Now he smells."

So why did the Lord delay? And why was the Lord in His tomb for three days? Because three days was the legal time required by Jewish law to make sure that the person was indeed dead. Martha knew that her brother's body would have a bad odour, to say the least, after four days, because it would have started to decay. But the Lord's body saw no decay, and I venture to say, had no 'bad odour'.

From the time of His birth, the Lord fulfilled the Law in every respect, and even in death, the Law's requirements were met. He rose from the dead after the three days. The fact that the Lord's body suffered no corruption in the tomb is another proof that He was indeed without sin.

# (13) Rising and ascending.

**The plan is complete.**

The death of the Lord on the Cross and His burial in the nearby tomb is not the end of the drama. There are, at least, still two acts to come.

The first is the Lord's resurrection from the dead. Please note, that as He needed a real body to carry out the first part of His work, resurrection also implies - really, it demands - that the Lord have a body. We know that His resurrection body was real, for He said to the disciples when He appeared to them for the first time after rising from the dead, "It is I myself! Touch me and see; a ghost does not have flesh and bones, as you see I have." He also ate a piece of fish as proof that He was real (Luke 24:39,42).

When the Lord rose from the dead, He was not, and is not now, a disembodied spirit. The Mediator who sits at the right hand of the Father in Heaven interceding for us is *the man Christ*

*Jesus* (1 Timothy 2:5), but now in His resurrection body.

The resurrection of Christ demonstrates beyond any doubt, that His life and sacrifice were perfectly acceptable to God. It also demonstrates that the power of death had been broken and that Satan is a defeated enemy. The resurrection is doubted by some Christians, and sometimes denounced outright, but it is an integral part of God's wonderful Plan.

Paul states in 1 Corinthians 15:19 that if Christ is not risen from the dead, then we believers are the most miserable of all people, for not only have we absolutely nothing to look forward to, but we go through this life thoroughly deluded. In verse 20, however, he proclaims the triumphant message that Christ has risen from the dead, and as the firstfruits of those who have fallen asleep, He leads the way for His redeemed people.

The Lord's resurrection guarantees that we will also rise from the dead and be clothed in our resurrection body as He was. What a wonderful prospect! We will have a body that is fitted for heavenly realms, eternal life that will carry us through whatever ages there are to come, and a place with Christ at the right hand of God assured by the power of the Word of God. Blessed indeed! Perhaps the most wonderful thing about that resurrection body is that, when we are clothed with it, we will then be able to serve and praise God as we should.

The second act that still had to take place is one that is easy to miss. I want you to come back to Leviticus 16 where we find the instructions for the Day of Atonement. Once again, we can only concentrate on the major points, so please read the chapter carefully.

This was the most solemn day in the Jewish religious calendar, and is full of teaching concerning the once-for-all sacrifice of the One who is both Sacrifice and High Priest. The first thing Aaron had to do on this day was to strip and wash himself thoroughly. He then put on linen garments that, though sacred, were not the usual splendid garments of the High Priest. After Aaron completed all he had to do in the Holy of Holies, he took off the linen garments, bathed himself again, and put on his usual robes. Leaving the linen garments behind, He then went out of the Tabernacle to the waiting people and carried out the final acts of this great Day.

I want you to notice in verse 17 that no one was allowed to be in the Tabernacle when Aaron was carrying out the acts of atonement in the Holy of Holies. In earlier instructions about the priestly duties, it is solemnly stated that once the priests and their utensils were consecrated, they could only be touched by consecrated hands. It would appear that at the crucial time, not even other priests were allowed near Aaron. Aaron himself was only tolerated by God in the sacred Sanctuary after he had undertaken special preparation, which included making several sacrifices and creating the cloud of incense. These precautions were "in case he die".

There are a number of high points in this very deliberate ceremony, so it is difficult to talk about one part as a climax, but perhaps we can say that the heart of it was the sprinkling of the blood on the "mercy seat", the golden lid of the Ark of the Covenant, to make atonement for the confessed sins of the people, sins which had been symbolically transferred to the sacrificial victims.

Did you notice I said "victims"? It had completely escaped my notice for a long time that Aaron had to go into the Holy of Holies and sprinkle blood on the mercy seat *twice*, not just once. First the blood of a bull, and then that of a goat. This means that he would have *come out* through the Veil twice, not once. And as we saw earlier, before he comes outside the second time and shows himself to the people, he changes back into his High Priestly robes.

Now what are some of the lessons we can learn from these things? Each Gospel gives different details of the Crucifixion, Resurrection and subsequent appearances of the Lord, and we must carefully compare these so we don't miss anything important. In John 20, from verse 10, we read of Mary Magdalene's encounter with the Risen Lord. It was when He said her name that she knew who He was. Mary's immediate reaction was to prostrate herself and grab hold of His feet. The Lord forbade this, saying, "Do not hold onto me, for I have not yet returned to the

Father." The *KJV* says, "Touch me not, for I am not yet ascended to my Father."

When the Lord stopped Mary from touching Him or holding onto Him, I want you to focus on the reason He gave. "I have not yet returned to the Father". Later in the day, He allowed other women to touch Him (Matthew 28:9), and in John 20, as well as in other Gospels, He invites the terrified disciples to touch Him, when He appears to them that same evening.

What is the inference? If Mary could not grab onto Him, early in the morning, because He had not yet returned to the Father, but later in the day He invites people to touch Him, it must be that, in the meantime, He had indeed returned to the Father. Why did He have to do that?

The Day of Atonement, and the Book of Hebrews, gives us the answer: to make Atonement and to cleanse the Heavenly Tabernacle. And just as everyone had to 'leave the premises', so that Aaron would not be contaminated by contact with anything unclean, in the same way, the Lord could not be touched or held onto by any sinful child of Adam. Mary, very understandably, wanted to hold onto her beloved Lord, but not only must He maintain His uncontaminated state, He also had a work to do that was His alone. He was the Lamb foreordained before the foundation of the world, and the wonderful redemption of God was not complete until the blood of that Lamb – the one and only Lamb – had been sprinkled on the Mercy Seat of the Heavenly Tabernacle.

Was the offering acceptable to God? Again Leviticus helps us out. When Aaron emerged from the Holy of Holies and showed himself to the congregation of Israel, they knew that the offering had been acceptable, their sins of the previous year had been atoned for and forgiven and they could start another year with a clean slate. So it was with the true High Priest. When He came back and showed Himself alive to His people, this was the signal that Atonement had indeed been made, and forgiveness and all its associated blessings, were freely available to sinful mankind. The big difference from the Old Testament type was that Christ's sacrifice *never needed repeating*.

The other aspect of Aaron's work on the Day of Atonement was to cleanse or purify the Tabernacle. This was because the Tabernacle was in the midst of sinful people. Even the priests, in spite of their ceremonial washings and sacrifices, contaminated it by their own sinfulness.

Did the Heavenly Tabernacle need cleansing? Yes, indeed it did. In Hebrews 9, after reading in verse 21 of the cleansing of the earthly tabernacle by the sprinkling of blood, we have in verse 23 these words:

> It was necessary, then, for the copies of the heavenly things (i.e. in the earthly tabernacle) to be purified with these sacrifices, but the heavenly things themselves (had to be purified) with better sacrifices than these. For Christ did not enter a man-made sanctuary that was only a copy of the true one; he entered heaven itself, now to appear for us in God's presence.

We can well understand how the earthly Tabernacle needed cleansing because of the sins of the people, but why would the heavenly Tabernacle need cleansing? We must go back again to Ezekiel 28. From verse 11 on, the words refer to the angel who became Satan. It would appear that he was in charge of the sanctuaries in Heaven, and may have been the "Master of the Worship of God". His adornment of precious stones is reminiscent of the high priest's robes, and verse 18 tells us that he desecrated the sanctuaries given to his charge. Isaiah 14:12-13 tell us that his sin was pride. He aspired to God's position and wanted to be worshipped as God.

Here is the sin that defiled the true Tabernacle in heaven. We tend to forget that the redemption of sinful humanity is not the complete goal of God. Our salvation is *part* of that goal, but the more important part is that God should finally be *all in all*. This requires, among other things, that the stain of Satan's sin and rebellion be wiped out, which was one of the reasons why the Lord had to go into the Heavenly Tabernacle after His resurrection, without being contaminated by any sinful contact.

So Satan was not only vanquished by the Cross and Resurrection and his doom sealed, but the blood of the innocent Lamb provided by God, also cleansed the Heavenly places of every stain left by the sin of the one who wanted to take God's place.

After carrying out these heavenly functions that the Day of Atonement prefigures, the Lord returned to His faithful followers and prepared them for the difficult and dangerous work that was ahead of them. He then ascended to His Father's side in Glory to await the moment when Israel will look on Him whom they pierced, and mourn. Then He will come forth, arrayed in His full regalia of power and glory, to save His people (Israel), crush their foes and set them in their long-intended position as the priests of God to the nations of the world.

# (14) Of all we have said ... This is the sum.

We have covered a lot of ground in our overview of the wonderful Plan of Redemption, yet I am so conscious of what has not been said. I want to repeat what I said at the beginning. God's Remedy for Sin is not a hit-or-miss affair, but a connected, unified and coherent scheme that needs each of its parts to succeed. I have found that as I have come to see and understand these different parts, and appreciate how they mesh one with another, I appreciate much more what God has done for me as a sinner. This brings up in me a stronger determination to serve Him to the best of my ability.

I must also repeat that we do not need to know all the things covered in this study to be saved. God, in His great wisdom, has made entry to salvation so simple that even a young child can take the step, as many of us can testify. But our salvation, I believe, should produce not only good works, but also growth in the knowledge of what it took to gain our salvation on God's part.

Our quest took us back before Adam, when rebellion rose in Heaven through the pride of Lucifer. This challenge to God's supremacy brought about the creation of Adam, a lesser being than the angels, who was tested as to his obedience to God, and failed. Satan probably thought he had won at that point, but the first Adam was a picture of another Adam who was still to come. Called Jesus, (the Greek form of the Hebrew name Joshua), He also came in the same lesser form, but when He was tested, was faithfully obedient.

Because of His unique birth and sinless life, He was the only man who could stand in the place of the first Adam and die the death that Adam should have died back in Eden. Because we are all 'in Adam', the Lord's death in Adam's place touches us all. First of all, it suspends the immediate imposition of the death penalty, as the sacrifices in Eden did for Adam and Eve, and gives all humanity the chance to turn to God in repentance and accept the forgiveness and life He offers all so freely in Christ. For those who do accept God's wonderful offer in faith, there is immediate forgiveness, and the conscience is free from guilt in a way that the animal sacrifices of the Mosaic ritual were never able to achieve. Many other blessings come to us as well. We enter into these things fully, not at our deaths, but at our resurrection, when our spirits that went back to God when we died, are united with our resurrection bodies. That is the way in which we will be forever with the Lord. As one of the members of our study group here in Newcastle, Australia, often says: "I don't believe in life after death. I believe in life after resurrection."

For those who reject God's offer, there is nothing to look forward to but judgement and the second death from which there is no escape or return.

It is too easy to ignore or underestimate what God had to do to bring His Plan of Redemption to completion, because, after all, nothing is too hard or impossible for God. I believe, however, that the 'illuminating experiences' we read in the Old Testament, such as the offering of Isaac by Abraham on Mt. Moriah, are not only to teach us the truth about some part of God's Plan, but also to give us some idea of what it cost God to carry out His Plan. I suppose that this is something each one has to come to individually. I pray that, in this sense especially, we shall all continue to grow in grace and in the knowledge of our Lord and Saviour, Jesus Christ.

# More on Salvation

If you have enjoyed this publication you may care to read the following:

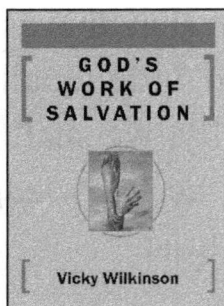

Salvation: God's Provision and Man's Response
By Brian Sherring

Seven Aspects of Salvation
By Brian Sherring

God's Work of Salvation
By Vicky Wilkinson

Further details of the books opposite
can be seen on

**www.obt.org.uk**

They can be ordered from that website
and from

The Open Bible trust,
Fordland Mount, Upper Basildon,
Reading, RG8 8LU, UK.

They are available as eBooks from
Amazon and Apple and also as
KDP paperbacks from Amazon.

# About the author

Athol Walter was born in November 1932 at Albany, Western Australia, of Salvationist parents. He was educated at Bunbury High School and, in 1954, entered The Salvation Army Training College for Officers in Melbourne, Victoria. In 1957 he married Eveline Palstra, who was also a Salvation Army Officer. Their ministry was mostly in country towns of Victoria. In January 1967 they resigned their ministry in The Salvation Army and moved to New South Wales to be part of the dispensational group in Sydney. After the death of the group's leader, George Collier, Athol was invited to become the leader. In subsequent years, the group became the Berean Bible Fellowship of Australia. He has been the President of the BBFA and is at the time of writing this book, he was the editor of its magazine *Spiritual Blessings*.

# Books on Christ

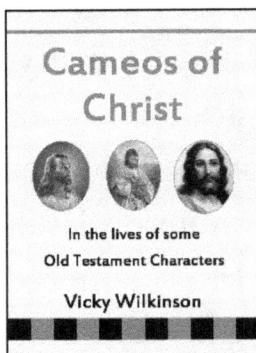

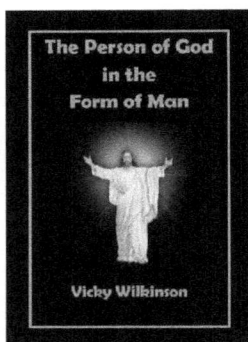

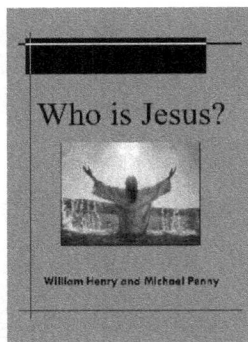

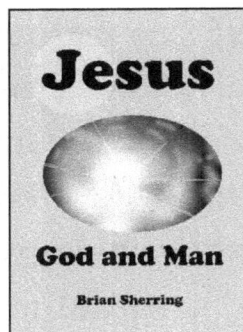

**Cameos of Christ**

In the lives of some
Old Testament Characters

Vicky Wilkinson

**In Christ and With Christ**

Vicky Wilkinson

PUT ON THE LORD
JESUS CHRIST

Vicky Wilkinson

**The Person of God in the Form of Man**

Vicky Wilkinson

Who is Jesus?

William Henry and Michael Penny

**Jesus**

**God and Man**

Brian Sherring

Further details of the books opposite
can be seen on

**www.obt.org.uk**

They can be ordered from that website
and from

The Open Bible trust,
Fordland Mount, Upper Basildon,
Reading, RG8 8LU, UK.

They are available as eBooks from
Amazon and Apple and also as
KDP paperbacks from Amazon.

# Free magazine

*Search* magazine is published bi-monthly by
The Open Bible Trust

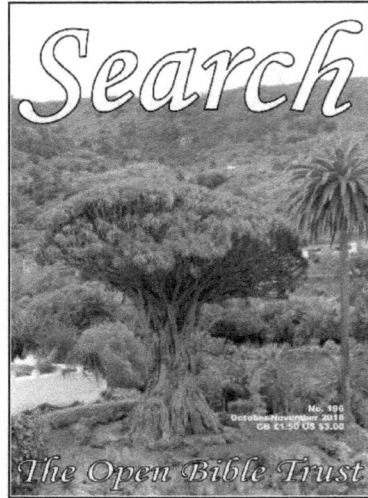

*That Wonderful Redemption*

# About this book

## That Wonderful Redemption
### God's Remedy for Sin

The question the unbeliever should ask is, "What must I do to be saved?" However … the believer should ask, "What did God have to do in order to save me?"

This book deals mainly with the second question. However, we do not need to know and understand all these things in order to be saved. God saves the sinner purely on the basis of faith in the Lord Jesus Christ's sacrifice for sin and His resurrection. But surely a desire to understand and know in part how it works must surely follow.

God's Plan of Salvation is made up of a number of parts, each one being necessary to the success of the whole. Moreover, if any one of the parts is absent or fails, then the whole scheme fails. It is this teaching that underlies what is presented here. However, it must be said that no matter how much we may come to know and understand how God's wonderful salvation works, we will never fully know it all, never completely understand it all, and will never be able to answer all questions. Moreover, there comes a time when all the studying and analyzing must stop, and we simply must bow in submission and adoration and appreciation before our great God and Saviour, Jesus Christ.

Publications of The Open Bible Trust must be in accordance with its evangelical, fundamental and dispensational basis. However, beyond this minimum, writers are free to express whatever beliefs they may have as their own understanding, provided that the aim in so doing is to further the object of The Open Bible Trust. A copy of the doctrinal basis is available on **www.obt.org.uk** or from:

**THE OPEN BIBLE TRUST**
**Fordland Mount, Upper Basildon,**
**Reading, RG8 8LU, UK.**

www.ingramcontent.com/pod-product-compliance
Lightning Source LLC
Chambersburg PA
CBHW070529030426
42337CB00016B/2163